HUDSON
TAYLOR

by
Susan Martins Miller

YOUNG READER'S CHRISTIAN LIBRARY

Illustrations by
Ken Save

A BARBOUR BOOK

Printed in the United States of America
ISBN 1-55748-338-8

Typeset by Typetronix, Inc.
Fort Myers, FL 33901

93 94 95 96 97 5 4 3 2 1

HUDSON TAYLOR

HE LOVED TO WATCH

1

The small boy sat very quietly, watching intently. His father gently and precisely measured powders and liquids and set them aside on the counter in his shop.

Hudson Taylor knew that his father had an important job—preparing the medicines that the doctors in Barnsley, England, wanted their patients to take. He also knew that he must not speak while his father was concentrating on the medicines. Still, he loved to watch. From time to time the bell on the shop door jingled and someone would come in to pick up a preparation. Hudson looked on proudly as his father gave instructions about how the medicine should be used. Between customers, father and son smiled at each other as if they had a secret known only to them.

Hudson turned his head as he heard a familiar creak and realized that his mother was coming through the door connecting the shop with the family's rooms behind it. The young woman saw her oldest child sitting so contentedly on the stool behind the counter she wished she did not have to disturb him. But the two parents had agreed that they would bring up their children to look after their own things and to develop the careful habit of repairing something as soon as it needed attention.

"There you are, Hudson," she said, smiling. "Have you been out here all afternoon? I never thought a five year old could be so interested in the work of a chemist!"

"THERE YOU ARE, HUDSON"

"I am interested, Mama, and I like to be with Papa." The boy's words were obviously sincere; Hudson's mother smothered a smile of amusement at how such a small child could be so serious.

"I noticed that the underarm seam of your nightshirt is a little loose. I think perhaps you ought to stitch it before it becomes a large hole."

"Must I do it now, Mama?" Hudson pleaded.

"Absolutely. The needle and thread are ready for you on your dressing table. If you need help, I'll be in the sitting room."

Hudson knew that it was pointless to protest further. Mama always insisted that he do these things right away. He hopped down off the stool and started toward his mother. When he heard his father speak, he stopped for a

"MUST I DO IT NOW, MAMA?"

moment to listen.

"I'm glad you came into the shop, dear," his father said. "I've invited some of the traveling ministers to tea this afternoon. It's been months since we had a good talk with any of them."

"Good! I look forward to visiting with them, too."

Hudson and his brother and sister were only little children but they loved to listen to the stories the preachers told from their trips all around England and several other countries. Standing in the doorway listening to his parents, he wanted to say how much he enjoyed the visits of the traveling Methodist ministers. Instead, Hudson glanced up at his mother and decided that he should go directly to his room to mend his nightshirt.

"GOOD...I LOOK FORWARD TO VISITING WITH THEM"

He had to stand on his tiptoes to see the top of his dresser and reach for the sewing basket. He carried it carefully to his bed, where he reached under his pillow for his nightshirt. Hudson knew right where the loose seam was; he had seen it for himself two days ago. He climbed up on the high bed, got comfortable right in the middle of it, and began making small, exact stitches in the fabric. As he sewed, he listened to his mother moving about the sitting room preparing for the guests who would be coming soon.

Mama always hid her own mending basket on the empty bottom shelf of the bookcase, behind the ruffled crimson curtain she had hung to brighten the room. The family's home was small, and Mama did not have all the pretty dishes that other mothers had, but

HE BEGAN MAKING SMALL, EXACT STITCHES IN THE FABRIC

Hudson felt very secure living there with his parents and his brother William and sister Amelia. Soon Mama would have another baby, and the rooms would become even more crowded, but Hudson did not mind.

Hudson was nearly finished mending when his sister Amelia, who was only three, came in with the exciting news that the traveling Methodist ministers would be coming to tea soon.

"I know that already," Hudson said, trying to act very old. "Papa told Mama while I was in the shop."

Amelia was clearly disappointed that Hudson had discovered this wonderful news and had not shared it with her immediately. He could see she was unhappy, so he added, "I would have told you right away, but Mama

"I KNOW THAT ALREADY"

sent me in to mend my nightshirt."

That seemed to make his little sister feel better, and she climbed up on the bed to sit next to him. But she climbed right down again when the shop doorbell jangled and she heard the voices of the guests they were waiting for. Hudson slid off the bed as quickly as he could, tucked his nightshirt under the pillow, returned the sewing basket to the dresser, and eagerly followed Amelia out into the sitting room.

His brother William, four years old, was already sitting quietly in one corner. The three children knew that they must not speak while their guests were talking, but the restriction never seemed to bother them. Papa and Mama would answer all their questions later. Right now, they were content to listen to the

RIGHT NOW, THEY WERE CONTENT TO LISTEN

adventurous stories the preachers told about the many people who believed in God and became Christians. Some of the men traveled around the country preaching all the time. Others, like Hudson's father, had other jobs to support their families and preached whenever they could. The best stories were from the guests who had been to foreign countries.

The pile of biscuits slowly disappeared, and the tea in the pot grew cold as the friends tried to catch up on all that had happened in the last few months. As he had in other meetings, Hudson's father brought the group's attention to one thing which weighed heavily on his heart.

"I don't know why the Methodists do not send any missionaries to China. There are millions of souls being lost each and every day in

"THERE ARE MILLIONS OF SOULS BEING LOST EACH DAY"

that great land. This is 1827, and we still have no Methodist missionaries in China." Papa would shake his head sadly, and others agreed with him. Still, at the next meeting there would be no report from China.

Hudson sat noiselessly until all the guests were gone, but he was very bothered by what his father had said about China. He hardly knew what China was, but he knew it was a very big country where people did not know about God, and this is what troubled his father.

The small boy, only five years old, crossed the room and put his hand on his father's knee. Papa looked at him and said, "Yes, Hudson? Do you have a question?"

"No, Papa, not a question. I just want to say that when I grow up I will be a missionary and I will go to China."

"I WILL BE A MISSIONARY AND I WILL GO TO CHINA"

"MY EYES ARE REALLY TIRED TODAY"

2

"Come on Hudson," George said, "It's quitting time."

"And I'm ready to quit," seventeen-year-old Hudson answered. "My eyes are really tired today." He rubbed both eyes with the heels of his hands, trying to rid them of the constant stinging sensation that had been bothering him for several weeks.

George reached across the desk to turn off the gaslight by which the two young men had been working. "I never thought there would be so much extra work at a bank," George said. "After all, we closed to the public several hours ago."

"Still, I like the work," Hudson said as they walked toward the door by the dim light of the street lamp outside.

George smiled. "It does you good to get out of your father's shop. He's spent the last seventeen years filling your head with a bunch of silly religious ideas. There is more to the world than Methodist preachers."

Hudson did not reply. It was true that his job as a junior clerk in the Barnsley bank had exposed him to many ideas his father disapproved of, and he had long ago stopped discussing these things with his family. He hated to have a wall in his relationship with his parents; they had always been a close family. Yet he felt the time had come for him to grow up and begin to think for himself. His friends at the bank had helped him to do that. Hudson

"THERE IS MORE TO THE WORLD THAN METHODIST PREACHERS"

was stimulated by their long philosophical discussions on politics, morality, and religion. At first he was eager to discuss religion and share his Christian upbringing. Gradually he began to spend more time listening. His new friends said things he had never thought about before, and he realized how sheltered his childhood had been. Perhaps his fellow clerks were right when they sneered at the traditional religious ideas his parents had taught him.

Hudson worked at the bank only a few months. The stinging in his eyes grew into a serious inflammation caused by the gas lights. Dismayed, Hudson had no choice but to resign and go back to working in his father's chemist's shop. Even working with his father, however, did not make Hudson forget the conversations at the bank. He longed to be on his

PERHAPS HIS FELLOW CLERKS WERE RIGHT

own, to earn his own money and spend his nights with his friends, perhaps even buy a horse to go hunting with them. Despite the effort his parents made to understand him, his discontentment continued.

One afternoon Hudson had a few hours off from his work in the shop and browsed through the books in his father's library looking for something to read. Nothing seemed to interest him until his eyes fell on a basket of pamphlets. He picked one up and flipped through a few pages. *Perhaps there is a good story here*, he thought. *I'll skip the sermon at the end*. He sat down to read the small book without any intention of taking it seriously. He was just looking for a way to pass the time.

But the book was more interesting than he

HE WAS JUST LOOKING FOR A WAY TO PASS THE TIME

had expected and he could not put it down. When the story ended and the sermon began, he kept reading about how the death of Christ on the cross at Calvary provided a full and perfect atonement for sin—even for his own sin. At first Hudson scanned over the paragraphs, telling himself that he had known this since he was a small child.

Suddenly he realized what this meant! If Christ's work was complete and the whole debt paid, what was left for him to do? A light flashed inside Hudson at that moment, and he could not resist the urge to fall to his knees and pray for this complete salvation he was reading about. All those years of instruction from his parents no longer seemed like a lot of silly religious ideas, as his friend George would think. Hudson was convinced that he

SUDDENLY HE REALIZED WHAT THIS MEANT

had come to the end of his search for truth. His mother and father had been right all along and had waited so patiently for him to realize this himself.

As excited as he was, Hudson kept his conversion a secret for several days. His mother was out of town, and he wanted her to be the first to know. But he was so excited, he found it too difficult to keep the news to himself that long, and he confided in his sister, Amelia.

"Oh, Hudson, that's wonderful!" Amelia was truly delighted. "I knew you were struggling to decide what you believed, and I have been praying for you three times a day for a month. I'm so glad to know my prayers have been answered."

"I never knew you were praying, Amelia. Thank you!" Hudson impulsively embraced

AMELIA WAS TRULY DELIGHTED

his sister, grateful for the part she had played in his new faith. "But please don't tell anyone. I want to tell Mother myself when she comes home next week."

When Mrs. Taylor walked through the door two weeks after Hudson's unforgettable day, he greeted her enthusiastically. "I have such glad news to tell you, Mother!"

She reached out and put her arms around his neck and held him close like she used to do when he was small. "I know, my boy," she said simply.

Hudson pulled back, very surprised and disappointed. He had not yet said what his news was. "Has Amelia broken her promise and told you?"

"No, Hudson, it was not from any human source that I found out. Two weeks ago I felt

"I KNOW MY BOY"

such a burden for your conversion that I got up from the dinner table and locked myself in my room. I was resolved not to leave that room until my prayers were answered. I prayed for hours, and that very day I felt the assurance that at last you knew my Lord for yourself."

The weeks that followed were a joyful time for the Taylor family. Amelia and Hudson went into the poorest parts of town on Sunday evenings to distribute pamphlets which would help others make the discovery Hudson had made that day in his father's library. They spoke with anyone who would listen and prayed for the people they met.

However, Hudson's quest to know the Lord was not over. As the weeks passed and the

AMELIA AND HUDSON WENT INTO THE POOREST PART OF TOWN

newness of his faith wore off he found himself feeling like he would rather sleep late instead of getting up early to read his Bible, and praying seemed like too much effort. Even as he felt this happening, Hudson did not like it. Surely God had more of a purpose for his life that this! He longed to be genuinely close to God, yet he felt unworthy to approach God. He continued to do things he knew were wrong, and the good things he meant to do somehow never got done.

For days and weeks Hudson could not figure out what was keeping him back. What could he do to rid himself of his sinfulness? He prayed constantly for God to show him what he should do. If only God would break the power of sin and allow Hudson to live a holy life, he would give himself completely to

IF ONLY GOD WOULD BREAK THE POWER OF SIN

whatever God wanted him to do. If only God would deliver him!

Hudson was startled when he thought he heard someone in the room with him—he had been sure he was alone. The room was dark, and he peered into the shadows to see who had entered. But no one was there. Hudson caught his breath as he realized that the presence he felt was God's presence. As he sat in awe he heard his prayer being answered as if God were speaking in a human voice. "Your prayer is answered. I will deliver you. Then go for me to China."

The young man, now seventeen, had long ago forgotten his childhood declaration that he would go to China. It was at this dramatic moment, during his unusual and spectacular meeting with God, that Hudson Taylor was

THE PRESENCE FELT WAS GOD'S PRESENCE

convinced that he would go to China as a missionary. This was the meaning of his months of spiritual struggle—to prepare him to say "Yes" to God's call. From that hour his mind was made up. Everything he did from that time on was to prepare him for the work God wanted him to do.

FROM THAT HOUR HIS MIND WAS MADE UP

HE KNEW HE MUST BE FULLY PREPARED

3

Hudson Taylor wasted no time getting ready to go to China. Immediately he decided to go beyond the chemist trade he had learned from his father and study medicine and go to China as a missionary doctor. He longed to go as soon as possible, but he knew he must be fully prepared.

He sat in the lecture hall during the day and pored over his medical books at night, pondering being a doctor in a foreign country. He would be far from his family, living in a land of strange traditions and a complicated language, thousands of miles away from anyone who would provide support for him. Though he had not yet been to China, he had read about the country and often tried to picture himself living among the people of that great land. He soon began to study the Chinese language in the leisure hours he had and to learn as much about the country as he could.

Hudson was still not satisfied that he was ready to go to China. He could prepare his mind by studying medicine and the Chinese language. He could prepare his body by maintaining good health. But he must also be prepared spiritually. Hudson was confident that God was able to provide whatever he needed at just the time that he needed it. His doubts were not about God but about himself. Did he have enough faith to trust God completely? During these years of preparation for a lifelong commitment to China, this was a serious question in his mind.

HE SOON BEGAN TO STUDY THE CHINESE LANGUAGE

Hudson was so hounded by this question that he looked for ways to test his own faith even while he was still living in England. He began working for a doctor as a part of his training. When they first met, Dr. Hardey said to Hudson, "I will pay your salary every three months. But you must remind me when it is due, because I am very forgetful and probably will not remember on time."

With a silent nod and a lump in his throat, Hudson recognized that here was an opportunity to test his faith. He decided right then that he would not remind Dr. Hardey when it was time for him to be paid. Instead he would pray that the doctor would remember. If Dr. Hardey forgot to pay him, then Hudson would trust God to provide the money he needed another way.

"YOU MUST REMIND ME WHEN IT'S DUE"

After several months, Hudson was due to be paid, but Dr. Hardey made no mention of his salary. Hudson stuck to his resolution and did not remind the doctor. Days passed, and Hudson found himself down to his last coin one Saturday night. This small amount was all the money he would have until Monday, when perhaps Dr. Hardey would remember to pay him. Hudson was not concerned. He always seemed to have what he needed, so he continued praying and thanking God for being faithful.

On Sunday evening of that weekend, Hudson was out distributing pamphlets in a very poor section of town. A ragged, weary man approached him and asked Hudson to come home with him and pray for his dying wife. He followed the man into his small, dark

HE ASKED HUDSON TO COME WITH HIM

room, where he saw five children huddled in one corner, their cheeks sunken and their eyes blank. It was clear that they were slowly starving to death. The man's wife was lying on a pallet on the floor with a newborn baby at her side, both of them obviously dying.

Hudson choked back tears as he looked around at this miserable family. As the children looked on he took the woman's hand and began to pray for her. As he struggled for words, he could almost feel the only coin he had burning a hole in his pocket. If only he had several coins he would gladly give them most of the money. As it was, he would have to give them everything he had or give them nothing.

The man had asked him to pray, so Hudson started praying. But his words were disconnected

HUDSON CHOKED BACK TEARS

and made no sense, even to Hudson. Finally the man broke in and said, "You see what a terrible state we are in, sir. If you can help us, please do!"

At that moment the words flashed into Hudson's mind, "Give to the one who asks of you." Slowly he reached into his pocket and closed his hand around his coin. He pulled it out and placed it in the man's hand. It was not a great deal of money, but he explained that it was all he had. The man was very grateful, for even a small amount of money would enable him to call the doctor to come and help his wife.

The next morning, Monday, Hudson ate the last of the porridge he had on hand. He had no more food in the house, no more money in his pocket, and no guarantee that Dr. Hardey

HE EXPLAINED THAT IT WAS ALL HE HAD

would remember to pay him. As he thought about his problem, he heard a knock on the door and was surprised when his landlady brought in a letter. Hudson was puzzled. He did not recognize the handwriting on the envelope, and the postmark had been smudged so he could not tell where the letter had come from. Swiftly he slit the corner of the envelope and reached in. Still puzzled, he unfolded the sheet of paper—only to find it was blank. However, wrapped inside the paper was some money—much more money than he had given away the night before. In all the years that followed, Hudson never knew who sent that package to him.

At least now he knew he would be able to buy food for a few more days. But there was still the problem that Dr. Hardey had not

WRAPPED INSIDE THE PAPER WAS SOME MONEY

remembered to pay him. Each day of that week Hudson struggled to keep his promise not to remind the doctor but only to pray for God to remind him. Over and over again he told himself that if he could not withstand this test of his faith, then he was not ready to go to China.

By Saturday Hudson was beginning to feel embarrassed. Not only was he out of food again, but his landlady would be expecting a rent payment. If he did not pay his rent, then she could not buy the things she needed for herself. The day crept by slowly. Hour by hour Hudson prayed silently for Dr. Hardey to remember his salary.

Finally, late in the afternoon, Dr. Hardey said, "By the way, Taylor, is not your salary due again?"

Hudson was overcome with emotion. The

"...IS NOT YOUR SALARY DUE AGAIN?"

doctor had remembered! He found that he had to swallow several times before he could even respond to the doctor. Keeping busy and looking away from Dr. Hardey, he said, "It has been overdue for some time now, sir." He felt such relief that his prayer had been answered he could hardly speak.

"Oh, I am so sorry that you did not remind me! You know how busy I am. I wish I had thought of it a little sooner, for only this afternoon I sent all the money I had to the bank. Otherwise I would pay you at once."

Hudson could hardly believe his ears. He was not going to be paid after all! Once again he swallowed hard and tried to control his emotions. His hand shook as he lifted some supplies off the counter, and he concentrated very hard on not letting Dr. Hardey see how

HE WAS NOT GOING TO BE PAID AFTER ALL

upset he was. Seeming calm outwardly and trying to appear as normal as possible, he slowly walked from the room.

When he returned to the room Dr. Hardey had left for the evening. Hudson sat down on a stool and let his shoulders sag. Should he have given in to the urge to remind Dr. Hardey to pay him? Was it fair to make his landlady suffer because he wanted to practice believing God? Confused, Hudson sat alone in the dark, praying for the right decision.

At ten o'clock that night, still with no clear answer in his mind, Hudson was ready to put out the light and go home. With his overcoat halfway on, he heard a noise and stopped to listen carefully. Dr. Hardey was walking very quickly—and he was laughing aloud. He burst into the room with a grin on his face and

HE WAS LAUGHING ALOUD!

explained to the puzzled young man. "One of my wealthiest patients just came by to pay his bill. I do not know what prompted him to come at this hour, but he has paid in cash. Here, take part of the money to tide you over and I will pay you the rest of your salary next week."

He was gone as quickly as he had come. Hudson stood in the doorway with his fingers wrapped around the bills the doctor had pressed into his hand. Standing alone in the dark, he said aloud, "I will be able to go to China after all."

"I WILL BE ABLE TO GO TO CHINA AFTER ALL!"

HE WAS SAILING FOR CHINA AT LAST

4

"September 19, 1853." Hudson Taylor, now twenty-one years old, wrote the date very carefully in his journal and described in detail all that had happened on that day. He was sailing for China at last.

He was finally able to answer fully God's call for him to take the Gospel to China. Although he had not quite finished his medical degree and had not been ordained, the Chinese Evangelization Society had felt he was ready to go to China as a missionary. On that early fall morning he boarded the *Dumfries*, a cargo ship, as the only passenger.

His full heart almost broke at the sight of his mother standing on the pier waving goodbye.

She had come aboard to be sure his cabin was adequate, and together they had sung a hymn and knelt in prayer. And then she had returned to the pier while he remained on board. Not until the very moment of parting from his family did Hudson understand the price they were all paying by his obedience to God's call.

After the ship lurched away from the dock Hudson closed his diary and looked around his small cabin. Being a passenger on a cargo ship was the least expensive way to get to China; it was not the fastest nor the most comfortable. The captain had told him the voyage could take as long as six months, and this confining space where Hudson now sat would be his home for that time.

He decided to go up on deck and watch the

THIS CONFINING SPACE...WOULD BE HIS HOME

land slide from his sight. In the quiet moments leaning over the rail he felt God's comfort and was confident he had made the right choice in going to China at this time.

Unfortunately the winds were not right for making progress with great speed. The *Dumfries* spent more than a week in the English Channel trying to make its way out to open sea. Finally, on the twelfth frustrating day the winds suddenly picked up. At first Hudson thought this was a good sign and was excited that his journey would at last be underway. But soon he realized that the captain was not as pleased with the increasing winds. Something was definitely wrong. Hudson watched as the able crew moved swiftly about the deck trying to capture the power of the wind. The sails flapped loudly as the muscular

SOMETHING WAS DEFINITELY WRONG

men pulled on the ropes and followed the orders shouted by the captain.

Soon it was clear that everyone on board was in serious danger. When Hudson saw the captain running across the deck toward the mainsail, he grabbed his arm and tried to stop him.

"Sir, please tell me what I can do to help!"

"Just stay out of the way, young man!" The captain roughly shrugged off Hudson's touch and sprinted once again toward the crew.

As Hudson stood watching, frustrated that he could not help, he lost his balance and nearly went over the rail. Rather than sending the ship out into the open sea, the wind, blowing at gale force, was moving the *Dumfries* toward a formation of huge rocks close to the coast. Enormous waves beat viciously against

THE WIND WAS MOVING THE DUMPHRIES TOWARD HUGE ROCKS

the side of the vessel, rocking it from side to side.

Hudson gripped the railing tightly now. He had seen the rocks for himself and understood the danger which threatened everyone. Ducking his head against the wind and pulling himself along the railing with two hands, he made his way toward the stairs which would take him down to his cabin. Once there, sheltered from the wind but still swaying from side to side, he managed to write out his name and address and put the small piece of paper in his pocket. His hope was that when his body was found there would be someone who could notify his family. Then he searched through his belongings for things that might float and tied these things together into a bundle.

Just as he did so, resigned to his own death

HE MADE HIS WAY TO THE STAIRS

without seeing China, the swaying seemed to slow down. Hudson felt the ship change direction; he grabbed his bundle and ran up the stairs to see what was going on. What he saw horrified him. They were nearly upon the treacherous rocks, yet the captain continued to try to turn the boat around—and was succeeding at last. In a few more minutes the turn was complete and captain and crew began to relax. A victorious shout went up from the men when they were sure that they were out of danger.

The journey continued smoothly for many weeks after that perilous beginning. Hudson discovered that there was a Swedish carpenter on board who was also a Christian and together they held regular worship services for the crew. By the time they reached New

A SWEDISH CARPENTER WAS ALSO A CHRISTIAN

Guinea two others had become Christians.

It was during a service off the coast of New Guinea that Hudson saw the captain repeatedly looking over the rail with an expression of concern. When Hudson asked the reason for his worried look the captain explained that the vessel was being carried toward sunken reefs that could destroy the ship and again endanger the lives of the crew. Using all his skill the captain did everything he could to avoid the reef, but at last he told Hudson there was nothing more to do.

"But Captain, there is more we can do." Seeing the captain's puzzled face, the young missionary continued. "There are four of us on board who are Christians. We will go to our cabins and pray for God's help."

"It can do no harm, Mr. Taylor. Do as you

"BUT CAPTAIN, THERE IS MORE WE CAN DO"

wish." The captain certainly expected nothing to come of their prayers, but he thought that the Christians might as well go to their deaths believing in their God.

Hudson and the three others did go to pray, each to his own cabin. But Hudson did not stay there long. After only a few minutes of prayer he was convinced that God would save the ship. He dashed back up to the deck and saw the first officer sitting at the base of the mainsail. There was absolutely no wind, and the ship was drifting ever closer to the threatening reefs.

"Sir!" Hudson cried out. "I beg you, let down the mainsail. Let the wind carry us out of danger."

"Are you mad, Mr. Taylor?" the unbelieving officer scoffed. "There is no wind. There is no

"ARE YOU MAD, MR. TAYLOR?"

point in letting down the sail."

At that moment the corner of the sail began to flap in response to a gentle breeze. Hearing the sound, the first officer jumped up and immediately began working the mainsail. Other members of the crew hurried to help. Soon the wind grew strong and steady, and the *Dumfries* was on its way back out to the safety of the open sea.

Hudson stood on the deck watching the flurry of activity and gave a prayer of thanks. Surely this faithful God would deliver him safely to the shore of China and generously provide for every need he faced in the task of preaching the Gospel to the Chinese people.

THE SAIL BEGAN TO FLAP IN RESPONSE TO A GENTLE BREEZE

HE COULD HARDLY BELIEVE HE HAD ARRIVED IN CHINA

5

Hudson stood before the gate to the missionary compound, where all the missionaries lived and worked, with one bag tucked under his arm and another slung over his shoulder. His heart was beating rapidly as he scanned the outside of the compound. This was the beginning of a whole new way of life for Hudson Taylor. Six months on the boat had made him very anxious to be here, but still he could hardly believe that he had actually arrived in China.

He had just walked more than a mile through the narrow, crowded streets of Shanghai and could hardly believe that he had made his way safely here with his limited understanding of Chinese. Many people in the streets had stopped to look at the strange Englishman who did not know where he was going. But at last he had found his way.

The tall spire of the chapel was the first thing Hudson saw that told him he was in the right place. Standing at the gate now, he could see that there was also a hospital and several houses. He hoped to find Dr. Medhurst, a famous and important missionary in China, and that Dr. Medhurst would be able to help him find a place to live and get started on his work.

Shyly, Hudson knocked on the door of the first house. He had spent six months on a voyage bringing him thousands of miles to this place, yet he was nervous about introducing himself to these people.

Hudson soon found that he did not need to be nervous. The door was quickly opened, and the

HUDSON KNOCKED ON THE DOOR OF THE FIRST HOUSE

missionaries graciously welcomed him. For many months it was difficult to find a house to live in on his own, so he lived with other missionaries, learning about the Chinese way of doing things. Although he had studied the Chinese language while he lived in England, Hudson needed to learn a great deal more before he would be able to live and work among the Chinese people the way he wanted to. Hour after hour he sat at the table in his room studying Chinese.

The other missionaries in the compound, although kind to Hudson, were very busy with their own work. Sometimes it was hard to concentrate in his room when he wanted to be out doing the work he had come so far from home to do. Hudson could hear the missionaries chattering in Chinese and see them walking up and

THE MISSIONARIES GRACIOUSLY WELCOMED HIM

down the streets with confidence and ease. He strained to listen carefully whenever he heard Chinese being spoken, struggling to make sense of the many complicated sounds which made up the language. Someday, he reminded himself, he would be ready to move about freely and confidently the way they did.

The beginning of Hudson Taylor's missionary work was also difficult because of political events in China. Soldiers were in the streets constantly, firing shots throughout the day as fighting broke out between those who supported the government and those who wanted to change it. Hudson was discouraged each day to look out his window or take a short walk and see the misery of the people around him. Soldiers of both armies tortured each other and stole food and supplies from anyone who had them.

SOLDIERS WERE IN THE STREETS CONSTANTLY

Hudson was in a perplexing and frustrating situation. He wanted to do medical work, but he had not finished his medical training, so he was not truly a doctor. He was used to preaching and praying for others, but he was not really trained as a pastor either. And the Chinese Evangelization Society which had sent him to China had not estimated very well what his expenses would be, and Hudson had almost no money to live on and no idea where he could get more. He had many, many opportunities to test the strength of his faith and to trust God to provide for him during these first lonely months in Shanghai.

At last an invitation came from another missionary for Hudson to go on an evangelistic trip. Hudson and Mr. Edkins set out on a Chinese

AN INVITATION CAME FROM ANOTHER MISSIONARY

houseboat for a week's journey. The anchors were drawn up and the sails hoisted and, with the help of the Chinese family who owned the boat, the two missionaries floated down the river, traveling forty miles south of Shanghai.

This was Hudson's first chance to really be out with the Chinese people, to see how they lived, to share in their lives. Although it was only for seven days, he was very excited and enthusiastically handed out Chinese literature throughout the city of Sungkiang.

Before leaving the city, Hudson and Mr. Edkins approached the massive gray pagoda of the Buddhist religion. The enormous structure had stood in that spot for 900 years. The priest in charge allowed them to enter the pagoda, and they climbed to a high point where they could look down on the entire city sprawled below

HE ENORMOUS STRUCTURE HAD STOOD... FOR 900 YEARS

Tears came to Hudson's eyes as he gazed out on the countryside. From this spot he could see literally thousands and thousands of homes of Chinese people where little was known about Jesus Christ. The villages and temples and cities stretched out before him, calling him once again to go live among the people, to care for their physical needs, and to tell them of the love of God. He remembered the day when he had heard God say, "Then go for me to China." Silently Hudson scolded himself for the depression and discouragement he had been feeling. God had called him here for a purpose, and standing here at the top of a Buddhist pagoda he once again felt the Lord's touch gently steering him toward the Chinese people.

Back in Shanghai, Hudson intensified his

GOD HAD CALLED HIM HERE FOR A PURPOSE

efforts at language study. Now that he had been out on one evangelistic trip he was more eager than ever to travel to other places in China with Christian literature and look for chances to talk to Chinese people. Before long Hudson was making regular trips to other ports along the coast, sometimes alone, sometimes with another missionary. More and more he saw that the ointments, powders, and pills he carried in his medicine chest were a way to capture the interest of the Chinese, who would then accept his pamphlets and small books as well. Over and over again he was overwhelmed by the enormous population of China—millions of souls waiting to hear about Jesus Christ.

By the end of his first year in China, Shanghai was at peace once again and the coastal area had become a comfortable place to continue

HUDSON WAS MAKING REGULAR TRIPS

missionary work. But Hudson was not satisfied. His eyes and heart turned toward the inland parts of China, away from the protected seaports. His soul burned with the burden of reaching these people, and he knew he could not rest until they too had received the Christian message.

HUDSON WAS NOT SATISFIED

"SHE'S SO BEAUTIFUL"

6

"She's so beautiful!" Hudson said, looking fondly at the gentle Maria Dyer as she gracefully served tea to the group of missionaries gathered in the city of Ningpo. He did not realize he had spoken aloud until his companion gave him a strange look. Abruptly, Hudson excused himself and drifted off to another part of the house where he could be alone with his thoughts.

For weeks he had been torn in two by his feelings for this lovely young girl. He had no proper home, practically no income, and a career which would demand sacrifice and hardship year after year. What right did he have to think of marriage at this time in his life? What right did he have to think Maria would even consider his offer? Despite everything, however, he loved her more and more every day and dreamed of telling her so. But he never had a chance to express his feelings. Although they met often in a group with other missionaries, Maria and Hudson rarely were alone together.

Slowly Hudson shuffled his feet back to the room where the group was drinking tea and sharing information about their work. When he reached the doorway he stood still, completely captivated by Maria's gliding steps and soft smiles.

After being in Ningpo for only three months, Hudson was called back to Shanghai. Certainly he would have preferred to stay in Ningpo and be near Maria, but he was needed

MARIA AND HUDSON WERE RARELY ALONE

in Shanghai. His new work gave him many opportunities for preaching in several places. While he was glad to be able to do this, Hudson was more lonely every week, missing Maria more all the time. After more than four months he decided to write to her and ask Maria Dyer to be his wife.

Hudson could hardly concentrate on his work as he waited for her response. The days passed slowly and more than a week went by. At last after two weeks Maria's letter arrived—in an envelope marked with the clear, pretty handwriting which he knew was hers. It was very brief:

Dear Mr. Taylor,
I am afraid that what you have suggested is completely impossible. If you

"WHAT YOU HAVE SUGGESTED IS COMPLETELY IMPOSSIBLE"

*have any gentlemanly feeling, then I know
you will refrain from troubling me on this
subject ever again.*

Maria Dyer

When Hudson read these harsh words he fell
into a chair, stunned. There was no doubt that
this was Maria's handwriting, but he could not
believe that these were her words! Although
they had not had very many chances to be together privately, he had felt sure that she was
as fond of him as he was of her. How could this
be? Hudson was devastated and bewildered as
he read the short letter over and over again,
searching for some understanding of why she
would write to him in such a curt tone.

His questions went unanswered. His heart
ached as he continued to preach in Shanghai.

HUDSON WAS DEVASTATED AND BEWILDERED

As the months passed his love for Maria never diminished, and it was with mixed feelings that he responded to a call to return to Ningpo. He could be near Maria, but it might make his heartache worse to be near her and not be able to speak to her. Would he ever know the reason she thought it was impossible for them to marry?

The first time Hudson saw Maria again in Ningpo she smiled sweetly and welcomed him back. "I'm so glad that you have returned to Ningpo," she said. "I trust you have been well during your time in Shanghai."

Hudson was so startled that she had even spoken to him that he stuttered before finally saying, "Yes, Miss Dyer, I have been well. Thank you." Maria's companion touched her

"I'M SO GLAD THAT YOU HAVE RETURNED TO NINGPO"

elbow and hurried her along, but Hudson could not help but notice that as she walked away she looked over her shoulder at him. Her face looked kind and gentle as always, with no hint of the harsh tone of her letter. Now he was truly puzzled.

Soon the mystery unraveled. The missionary grapevine buzzed with speculation about what *was* going on between Hudson and Maria, and it was not long before Hudson learned, to his great joy, that Maria had been thrilled with his letter of proposal. However, the director of the school where she worked considered Hudson unworthy of Maria and had instructed her to write the letter Hudson had received. All these months, while Hudson was in Shanghai longing to be with Maria, she was in Ningpo hoping that he would return.

NOW HE WAS PUZZLED

One sultry afternoon in July, Hudson entered the house of a friend and discovered that Maria was also present. Hudson and Maria smiled secretly at one another as they realized that their friends had arranged for them to see one another. On the spur of the moment, Hudson decided that he would waste no time finding out how she felt about him.

"Miss Dyer," he began. "I wanted to ask you . . . ." Although he had rehearsed the words over and over in his head, Hudson found it difficult to speak.

"Yes, Mr. Hudson?" Maria said, looking at him coyly with a hint of encouragement in her voice.

Hudson had learned that Maria had an uncle in England who would have to give permission before they could marry, and he had

"YES... MR. HUDSON ?"

intended only to ask if he might write to her uncle. However, he wanted to know so much more from Maria.

"Miss Dyer. Maria. I love you. I have loved you for a long time, and I want to marry you!"

Now he had said it. Sitting face to face, he hoped she could give him an honest answer. Maria was smiling, but she was silent. Breaking out in laughter, Hudson realized he had not yet asked her if she would marry him.

"Miss Dyer, will you consent to be my wife?"

"Mr. Taylor, that would give me great pleasure."

They grinned broadly at each other, hardly aware that there were others in the room. All of the misconceptions of the past few months spilled out as they were joyously reunited.

"MISS DYER, WILL YOU CONSENT TO BE MY WIFE?"

Maria gladly agreed that Hudson write her uncle in England. They would wait together for the four months it would take for a response to reach them.

On January 20, 1858, a day filled with brilliant sunshine in Ningpo, China, Maria Dyer and Hudson Taylor were married. Hudson wore traditional Chinese clothes, and Maria wore a simple gray silk gown and wedding veil. At long last their prayers were answered and their hearts full of gratitude to God.

Two and one-half years after their wedding, after seven years in China, Hudson was exhausted and his health was poor. Maria and Hudson decided it was time to take their little daughter, Gracie, and return to England for physical rest. While they were there they would also try to find more missionaries willing to go to China.

MARIA DYER AND HUDSON TAYLOR WERE MARRIED

THEY HAD COME HOME TO ENGLAND

7

When Hudson and Maria stored away their meager worldly goods, bundled up little Gracie, and boarded the ship headed for England in 1860, they had no idea it would be nearly six years before they returned to their beloved China. As delighted as they were to be among friends and family in England, their thoughts and hearts were always far away in Shanghai and Ningpo and other places where their work had taken them. They had come home to England to refresh their health and to appeal for others to join them in their work. Without any hard feelings on either side, Hudson had separated from the Chinese Evangelization Society which had originally sent him to China. The Society, with its strict procedures and limitations, confined itself to the coastal towns of China. The burden burning in the hearts of Hudson and Maria was to evangelize the inland areas of that great country.

Their time in England was well spent. Together with a Chinese Christian who had accompanied them on their voyage, Hudson worked on a revision of the Chinese New Testament. He was also invited to write various articles about China and its needs. He was very glad to do this since his articles and the talks he gave would surely interest others in the work being left undone in China. During these years five workers were recruited and sailed for China even though the Taylors could not yet return themselves. Hudson and

...WORKED ON A REVISION OF THE CHINESE NEW TESTAMENT

Maria also added three little sons to their family during these years.

Despite progress in all these areas, in 1865, after being in England for five long years, Hudson was discouraged, wondering if there would ever be enough missionaries for China. Rather than increasing, the number of Protestant missionaries in China was dropping every year, and those who were there generally stayed close to the coastal towns. Very few ventured into the heart of the country.

Maria could only stand by and watch her husband withdraw. She tried to let him know in quiet ways that she would gladly listen if he wanted to talk, but he only seemed to keep to himself more and more. For several months he slept only an hour at a time during the night. Maria tried to keep the four small

HE ONLY SEEMED TO KEEP TO HIMSELF MORE AND MORE

children from bothering their papa too much and continued the family's routine as cheerfully as possible.

When the invitation came for them to spend time at Brighton, a sea town, Maria was delighted. Surely this was just was Hudson needed!

As soon as they arrived at Brighton, little Gracie ran squealing across the sand. "Papa! Papa! Take me to play in the water! Please! Please!"

Hudson could not help smiling down at his adorable daughter. But he did not feel ready to play in the water with the children. He stroked her fine hair as he explained, "We'll have plenty of time for that, Gracie. Right now, Papa wants to take a walk by himself. Would that be all right?"

"PAPA! PAPA! TAKE ME TO PLAY IN THE WATER!"

It was a bright Sunday morning when Hudson yanked off his shoes and socks, rolled up his pants, and let the sand ooze between his toes and then be washed away by the gentle tide pulling back out to sea. It was a perfect, peaceful picture—except that Hudson did not feel peaceful. Even coming to Brighton had not eased his inner torment. His steps quickened and he began to run along the edge of the water.

Over and over again, he reminded himself that he had no funds to support the missionaries he wanted to send to China. If he asked people to go, they would face danger and perhaps starvation. Was that fair?

He knew he was too ill to try to run in the sand. Maria would surely scold him if she saw him. Yet he kept moving, his thoughts

HUDSON DID NOT FEEL PEACEFUL...

churning and swirling constantly. Even if the missionaries did die of starvation, they would go straight to heaven, and if just one Chinese was saved, wouldn't that be worth the sacrifice? But could he really ask missionaries to make that sacrifice?

Exhausted, Hudson sank down in the sand and rested against a piece of driftwood. The sun was shining brilliantly, and he closed his eyes and leaned his head back. The warmth of the day seeped into his skin and he almost felt that he could give in to his desperate need for sleep.

Suddenly he sat bolt upright. If these missionaries went to China, it would not be because Hudson Taylor asked them to go. It would be because God himself asked them to go. Sitting in the sand with no one to hear

IT WOULD BE BECAUSE GOD HIMSELF ASKED THEM TO GO

him, Hudson said aloud, "Why, if we are obeying the Lord, the responsibility rests with Him, not with us!"

He raised his hands and looked to the sky. "The burden is Yours, Lord! As Your servant, I will continue to work, leaving the results to You!"

Hudson now felt immense relief. The burden was no longer on his shoulders—it never had been! The five missionaries whom he had sent to China were doing the work of the Lord, not the work of Hudson Taylor. The conviction he felt about evangelizing inland China was a conviction from God Himself.

With the ocean waves breaking at his feet and the sun beaming down on his shoulders, Hudson took a pencil and his Bible from his pocket. He found a clean spot in the margin

"THE BURDEN IS YOURS, LORD!"

and wrote simply, "Prayed for twenty-four willing, skillful laborers at Brighton, June 25, 1865." Twenty-four new missionaries, including those recently gone to China, would work in teams of two to reach the remote parts of the country.

With renewed energy, Hudson took long strides in the sand toward the house at Brighton where his family and friends were waiting for him. When Maria saw him coming she knew immediately that something tremendously important had happened. They stayed up long into the night talking in excited, hushed voices about what this experience would mean for their family and for the work in China.

First thing in the morning, Hudson went into London and, with a small deposit,

SOMETHING TREMENDOUSLY IMPORTANT HAD HAPPENED

opened a bank account in the name of China Inland Mission.

Maria and Hudson stayed in England for almost another year, spurred on by their goal of returning to China with enough teams to reach into the inner areas rather than staying in the safety of the coast. Hudson completed work on an influential book, *China's Spiritual Needs and Claims*, which attracted many people to his cause. The bank account opened in such a humble manner grew through generous contributions at a rate more rapid than anyone could have imagined.

On May 26, 1866, the Taylors and their four children were accompanied by one married couple, five single men, and nine single women when they boarded the ship

ON MAY 26, 1866...THEY BOARDED THE SHIP

called the *Lammermuir* and sailed once again for China.

The China Inland Mission had been born of faith on a sunny Brighton day.

THE CHINA INLAND MISSION HAD BEEN BORN OF FAITH

HUDSON AND MARIA RETURNED TO CHINA WITH GREAT DREAMS

8

Hudson and Maria returned to China with great dreams and a driving desire to tell the people of inland China about Jesus Christ. They set up the offices of the new China Inland Mission in their own home and settled the missionaries who had sailed with them into various provinces around the country. The mission work was on the threshold of a new era.

The early years of the mission were difficult years for the Taylors, however. By the summer of 1867, the thermometer frequently read over 100 degrees, even inside the house. The children were cranky and became sick easily. Maria took the children for a rest in the cooler countryside, and for a while it seemed they were all better.

But then little Gracie, their oldest child, grew ill and began to get weaker each day.

Hudson sat at her bedside, gazing down on his precious daughter and stroking her hot forehead. When at last she fell asleep Hudson picked up pen and paper and wrote a letter to a friend in England who was supporting his missionary work. He could not help but pour out his heart to his friend, writing: *I am striving to write a few lines from the side of a couch on which my darling Gracie lies dying. Yet God is faithful and strong, and we depend on Him.*

In only a few days, Gracie died. Wracked with grief, Hudson wrote to his mother: *Our dear little Gracie! How we miss her sweet voice in the morning, one of the first sounds to greet us when we woke. Is it possible that I shall never again feel the pressure of that little hand, never more*

IN ONLY A FEW DAYS, GRACIE DIED

hear the sweet prattle of those dear lips, never
more see the sparkle of those bright eyes? Yet I
know she is with Jesus, and would not wish her
back with us.

Maria and Hudson laid their sweet daughter to
rest, rejoicing that she was now with Jesus.
Casting aside any thought of being discouraged
because of their loss, they threw themselves into
the work of the China Inland Mission.

Just two years later it became clear that the heat
was again a threat to the health of the children.

"Hudson," Maria said, "We must decide what
to do about the children. We dare not risk another summer here for them."

Hudson shook his head sadly. "Yes, I know.
Little Samuel especially is very delicate. We
must send them back to England."

"I know you are right, dear," Maria said with

"WE MUST SEND THEM BACK TO ENGLAND"

catch in her voice. "Samuel is only five years old. How will we bear being apart from our children?"

Hudson put his arms around his wife and stroked her soft hair. "Our children are a gift from God. He has called us to this work in China, but we must also do what is best for them." Maria nodded silently as her husband continued: "Emily Blatchley has volunteered to return to England with the children so that you can remain here with me."

Maria looked up at Hudson and tried to smile. "I will be so much happier knowing they are with Emily." She wiped away a tear. "But Charles is too little to send. He should stay here with us."

"Then it's settled," Hudson said with determination. "I'll talk to Emily tomorrow."

"OUR CHILDREN ARE A GIFT FROM GOD"

As the time grew nearer for the four oldest children to return to England, Samuel fell ill. Once again Maria and Hudson looked on, helpless to heal their beloved son, trying only to keep him comfortable. It was only a matter of days before he fell into a deep sleep from which he did not awaken.

The summer brought more than intense heat. China was facing another political crisis with the threat of imminent war. Sickness ravaged many of the missionary families, and Maria insisted on pressing on alone—past the soldiers—to reach one family where death was near. Having suffered the loss of two of her own children, her heart reached out to the young missionaries as she nursed them and prayed for them to return to health. Satisfied that they would get well, she returned to Hudson and their

MARIA INSISTED ON PRESSING ON ALONE

small son, Charles, where she received the good news that her other children had reached England safely.

Soon after this, Maria herself fell ill with cholera. As she lay in her bed, she would imagine the children taking cool, green walks around the pleasant lake in England where they were living. At the peak of the July heat Maria gave birth to another son, and she welcomed him with great joy and love. However, she was so weak from her own illness that she could not feed the new little one. Soon the baby was sick, too. After only one brief week of life, during which he gave great joy to his mother, tragedy once again struck the Taylor family and the child died.

Weak as she was, Maria chose the hymns she wanted to be sung at the little funeral. No one guessed how gravely ill Maria really was as

TRAGEDY ONCE AGAIN STRUCK THE TAYLOR FAMILY

she stood at the grave. As soon as the service ended, she went back to bed to try to recover her strength.

Hudson sat by her bedside constantly. She did not seem to be in pain, but Maria was extremely weak and tired and was showing no signs of improvement. As she grew worse Hudson stayed with her all night, and as the new morning dawned he could see what the darkness had hidden—Maria was very near death. As he realized this, he could feel his own heart tearing.

"My darling," he said, "do you know that you are dying?"

"Dying!" she replied. "What makes you think so?"

Hudson could hardly speak, but he felt he must go on. "I can see it, darling. Your strength is giving way."

"MY DARLING... DO YOU KNOW THAT YOU ARE DYING?"

"But I feel no pain, only weariness."

"You are going home, Maria. You will soon be with Jesus."

"I am so sorry," she said softly.

Hudson spoke even more gently now. "Surely you are not sorry to go to be with Jesus."

"Oh no! It is not that. You know, darling, that for ten years there has not been a cloud between me and my Savior. I cannot be sorry to go to Him. But it does grieve me to leave you alone at such a time."

Maria and Hudson spoke few words after that. Having accepted that the end was near, they simply sat together as she drifted into unconsciousness. When the summer sun rose higher, Hudson heard the sounds of the city, coming to life for another day, contrast with Maria's labored breathing. Just after nine o'clock in the

"IT DOES GRIEVE ME TO LEAVE YOU ALONE "

morning she stopped breathing. Though he truly believed that she was at rest in the arms of Jesus now, he was stabbed with the pain of loneliness and silence. In only three short years he had witnessed the deaths of his daughter, his two sons, and now his beloved Maria. His older children were thousands of miles away in England, and he was left alone in China with motherless little Charles.

Many people would have understood if Hudson Taylor had decided to leave China and return to England permanently. Surely he had sacrificed enough for this enormous country. Yet Hudson never wavered in his conviction that God had called him to China and that there was still a great deal of work that God meant for him to do. Even though his heart ached intensely for his wife, who had been companion

HE WAS LEFT ALONE IN CHINA

worker, he never let go of his dream for inland China. Instead it intensified. He wanted to press on with the vision he had shared with Maria—to take Christ into the very heart of China.

HE WANTED TO PRESS ON WITH THE VISION

HE LOOKED FORWARD TO SOME PEACEFUL WEEKS

9

The year 1870 had been a very dark time in Hudson Taylor's personal life. Even amid tragedy after tragedy he pressed on in his work with the China Inland Mission. After twelve years of understanding companionship, he missed Maria every day. And he missed his three older children who were living in England. Late in 1871 Hudson decided he would visit England to attend to some business for the struggling China Inland Mission and to be with his children. He arranged to travel on a steamer and looked forward to some peaceful weeks of meditation and quiet thinking on the open seas.

He stood on the deck of the ship one day early in the voyage, watching the wake churn and foam as the boat hummed along. Lost in thought, he was hardly aware of the other passengers as they passed by chattering and gesturing in their own conversations.

"Mr. Taylor! Why, Mr. Taylor, I had no idea you would be traveling on this ship."

Surprised to hear his name, Hudson turned and looked up at the familiar young face with a friendly smile. "Miss Faulding, what a pleasant surprise. I thought you had left for England several weeks ago." Jennie Faulding had been a friend to Maria and Hudson for many years as they worked with the common goal of spreading the Gospel in China.

"I am due for a few months in England, but the work in Hangchow delayed my departure unexpectedly. Are you going home to see your children?"

"MISS FAULDING, WHAT A PLEASANT SURPRISE"

"Yes, and to look after some Mission business. It will be a delight to share the voyage with such a good friend as you have been."

Jennie and Hudson were together much of the time during the next weeks. They strolled around the deck for exercise, shared a table a mealtime, sat together for long quiet talks, and sometimes simply enjoyed a comfortable silence between them. They had been friends in China for many years, and now their friendship ripened into love. By the end of the voyage they had decided to be married as soon as possible.

The new Mrs. Taylor shared the intensity of Hudson's devotion to inland China. During their months in England, they often sat before a large map of China in their living room and prayed and planned for penetrating the interior of China. There were millions of Chinese who had

THEIR FRIENDSHIP RIPENED INTO LOVE

never heard of Christ: They must be reached! Hudson and Jennie met with others who were interested in the work of the China Inland Mission, and established a council which would manage the daily business of the Mission in England, handling financial donations and interviewing people interested in being missionaries to China. Jennie and Hudson were able to return to China with a sense that the Mission was being well taken care of in England.

"I have been looking forward to this trip for a very long time, Mr. Judd," Hudson said to his companion. "We have achieved our goal of establishing a center in Wuchang; now we have an opening into western China." The two missionaries were walking down the ship's ramp. Hudson wanted to make one last check on Mr.

"...NOW WE HAVE AN OPENING INTO WESTERN CHINA"

Judd's living quarters before leaving him to handle the work in Wuchang on his own.

"Watch out, Mr. Taylor!" shouted Mr. Judd. But it was too late. Hudson lost his footing and lay sprawled on the ramp looking stunned and embarrassed.

"Are you all right, sir? Perhaps you ought not to move just yet."

Hudson looked up into the anxious face of his friend and tried to put him at ease.

"I'm sure I'm quite fine, Mr. Judd. I seem to have twisted my ankle a little, that is all. Why don't you help me up and we'll see about it."

Mr. Judd locked his arms around Hudson and lifted him gently to his feet. Hudson began to wince immediately and hopped on one foot. "Perhaps we had better find a place to sit down, Mr. Judd."

"WATCH OUT, MR. TAYLOR!"

They moved together over to a crate and Hudson sat down. Reluctantly, Hudson admitted his pain. "Perhaps you should go find the ship's doctor."

The sudden fall on the gangplank had serious consequences. In addition to the injured ankle, Hudson experienced severe back pain and could move around only with the aid of crutches. Two months later, while he was still in great pain, news reached him that Miss Emily Blatchley, who was taking care of his children and looking after the Mission in England, had died. Despite his deteriorating physical condition, Jennie and Hudson set out for England immediately.

In England, Hudson's injury was diagnosed as "concussion of the spine," a condition which gradually developed into paralysis. Within a few weeks, Hudson could not move his legs at

"PERHAPS YOU SHOULD GO FIND THE SHIP'S DOCTOR"

all; in fact, he could not even sit. The doctor's orders were for him to stay in bed and rest. Still his condition worsened. At last he could only turn from side to side in the bed, and even that took great effort. He could not even hold a pen to write his own letters. He faced the possibility of never walking again.

In circumstances which would have dismayed and discouraged most other people, Hudson Taylor kept his thoughts fixed on the work in China. "Jennie, I need a map," he said one day.

She looked at him in surprise. "A map?"

"Yes, a map of China. I want to be able to see it from the bed. Our work is not finished."

Jennie smiled to herself as she fastened the map to the wall. She should have known that Hudson would persist no matter what the obstacles were. Patiently, she wrote the letters he

"OUR WORK IS NOT FINISHED!"

dictated and read to him from the Bible. Daily they prayed together for missionaries to go to China.

There were still nine provinces in China with no missionaries. The China Inland Mission was extremely low in funds and the flow of people asking about the work had trickled off. Hudson and Jennie had been praying for over two years for missionaries to these last nine provinces. He could not hold a pen, but Hudson could still speak the sentences which God put in his heart. Early in 1875, a pamphlet, "Appeal for Prayer on behalf of more than a hundred and fifty millions of Chinese," was published. In this short book, Hudson did not directly ask people to be missionaries. Rather, he simply asked them to join him in praying for eighteen missionaries to form nine teams to reach the inland

DAILY THEY PRAYED TOGETHER

provinces of China.

The response was overwhelming! Jennie brought in stacks of letters every day.

"Hudson, we must have help," she insisted. "We cannot keep up with the mail on our own."

Hudson nodded his agreement. "You are right, of course. We need people to help answer letters and arrange interviews."

Although Hudson was still confined to bed, he worked at a furious pace. Every moment of the day was taken up with responding to letters with the help of volunteers, with prayer meetings, with Council meetings, with interviews with potential missionaries.

It was not long before the eighteen missionaries Hudson had prayed for sailed for China. And still the flow of letters continued. More than sixty people volunteered to go to China, and the

"HUDSON, WE MUST HAVE HELP!"

money needed by the China Inland Mission came to them in strange and miraculous ways.

Ten years had passed since that day on the beach at Brighton when the China Inland Mission was born. They were years full of personal tragedy and spiritual challenge. And now Hudson Taylor, though lying flat on his back and in pain, gave glory to God for the spread of the Gospel across China.

HUDSON TAYLOR ... GAVE GLORY TO GOD !

HE RETURNED TO FULL HEALTH

10

The China Inland Mission was not the only subject of prayer among those who gathered around Hudson Taylor's bedside. One after the other, friends came to call and assure him they were praying for his recovery. Hudson himself seemed unconcerned about his own health: God had accomplished great things for the Mission even though its leader lay helpless. The prayers of those who loved Hudson were answered, and he returned to full health and was able to go once more to China.

After years of unfailing prayer and determined effort the China Inland Mission now stood on the threshold of a great opportunity—one which no other missionary organization had ever faced. So far, the missionaries in each province were traveling missionaries, and now the Mission had the opportunity to establish permanent mission stations in many of the provinces. The money needed to accomplish this was not coming in at a very fast rate, but Hudson never stopped believing that God would provide for his workers.

"We must go on," he would say to Jennie or to anyone who would listen. "We have always acted on faith, and we must not turn back now. God has opened too many doors to let us be stopped simply because of money."

Walking in the hills of Wuchang in 1882, Hudson pondered the problem. He counted in his head the number of workers needed to meet the most pressing needs. He pictured place after place and thought of the millions of Chinese still

HUDSON PONDERED THE PROBLEM

to be reached. "Seventy," he said aloud, though he was alone. "The Lord sent the seventy out, two by two, and we shall do this also."

Hudson hurried back to share this idea, which he believed the Lord had put into his mind, with his coworkers. At first, some of them thought this was impossible. "Even if we could find that many people willing to come," one said, "how would we raise the money we need for all those missionaries?"

"God will provide the workers and the money," Hudson insisted. Anyone looking at him could see that he believed sincerely what he was saying. "It is God who will send the people and He will know what they need."

The group held several prayer meetings and started discussing Hudson's contagious idea. Gradually Hudson's sense of excitement caught

"GOD WILL PROVIDE THE WORKERS AND THE MONEY".

on. It would take a lot of faith to ask God for that many people and that much money. They asked themselves, "Do we have the faith to believe God will do it?" Eventually they decided it would be realistic to plan to expand the missionary work over a period of three years.

"If only we could meet again and have a united praise meeting when the last of the seventy has reached China," suggested one missionary.

"We shall be widely scattered then," said another. "Why not have the praise meeting now? Why not give thanks for the seventy now?"

And so the band of missionaries held a meeting thanking God for the seventy new workers before even one of them had arrived on Chinese soil.

Although the Mission was not without problems, the work continued to expand. In 1886, Hudson suggested that the Mission plan to

"WHY NOT GIVE THANKS FOR THE SEVENTY NOW?"

accept 100 new missionaries in 1887—in one year! Again, some raised the objection of the cost, and again Hudson responded by repeating how urgent the need was to reach the millions of Chinese people who still had not heard the name of Christ.

The energetic leader of the Mission set out on yet another voyage to England to help find the workers needed for China. He made three visits to nearby Ireland and four to Scotland speaking on the subject of evangelizing the world. He also spoke at more than twenty conferences and retreats in England. Everywhere he went, he asked people to pray for the hundred to come forward.

And they did come forward. They came from all corners of England, Ireland, and Scotland. More than 600 people offered themselves as

HE SPOKE AT MORE THAN TWENTY CONFERENCES

candidates, and Hudson was overwhelmed with requests for interviews. He and his committee were careful to select only those who were completely dedicated to serving the Lord and who fully understood the harshness of life in China.

At the same time, others prayed and worked for the funds needed to send these volunteers on this voyage which would change their lives. Miraculously, the money was raised. In November of 1887, Hudson Taylor stood before the friends of the Mission and announced that God had given the hundred for which they had been praying—and that all the money they needed was available for all of them to go.

Because of one man's simple and constant obedience the China Inland Mission was now a major missionary force in China.

GOD HAD GIVEN THE HUNDRED

HUDSON TAYLOR WAS ANXIOUS TO RETURN TO CHINA

11

First, Hudson Taylor had prayed for twenty-four workers.

Then he heard the Lord telling him to find the seventy.

And then, though it seemed impossible, he was challenged to find the hundred.

And now the thousand began to come forward and offer themselves to the mission work in China.

After traveling throughout England, Scotland, and Ireland, Hudson Taylor was anxious to return to China. He had already made six trips to that vast country, and though he was no longer a young man, he wanted to go again. Hudson knew he had to return to England from time to time to find workers and raise the money needed for them to go to China, and of course he always enjoyed the opportunity to visit with friends and family. His children were grown, and it gave him great satisfaction that one of his sons was a missionary to China. He was very pleased with the growth of the Mission, which had already gone unbelievably far beyond his early dreams.

But in spite of this amazing progress, Hudson missed being among the Chinese people personally. While others began to see him as a great leader, Hudson continued to think of himself as a simple, humble missionary wanting only to obey God.

Hudson and Jennie continued to work together in many ways at the Mission headquarters. Their years together, working side by

HUDSON AND JENNIE CONTINUED TO WORK TOGETHER

side, had been very productive. Dozens of letters arrived each day from people interested in knowing more about the China Inland Mission, and dozens of invitations arrived with requests for Hudson Taylor to speak to large groups of people.

Jennie sat looking through the towering stacks of mail, as she did most mornings. With two particular letters in her hand she turned to her husband, who was bent over his own work.

"Hudson, what about these letters inviting you to visit North America?" she asked. "Should you consider going? Mr. Moody and Mr. Erdman are so determined; they feel they simply must have you speak at their conventions this summer."

Hudson sighed. "They are very kind to invite

"HUDSON, WHAT ABOUT THESE LETTERS...?"

me, but I have had no assurance from the Lord that the work should be extended by traveling to America. And I am anxious to return to China."

"Perhaps you should reconsider." Jennie turned back to her work without saying anything more. There was no need to pressure her husband. Hudson would listen to God's voice and do just exactly what he should do.

Although he had already turned down an invitation to visit America, Hudson could not keep ignoring the persistent letters. He thought and prayed some more.

"Jennie," he said a few days later, "I will go to America after all. I believe now that the Lord has a special reason for the repeated invitations I have received."

Jennie simply smiled and agreed.

"PERHAPS YOU SHOULD RECONSIDER..."

In the end, Hudson made plans to visit America and speak at several meetings on his way back to China in the summer of 1888. To his delight, his son and daughter-in-law decided to travel with him. Before he left on this important voyage, he stood before the yearly meeting of the China Inland Mission in London. His message had a simple point: "God is moving; are we also moving? Are we ready to go with Him?"

Hudson's challenging words rang in his own ears during the weeks he spent in the United States and Canada. He spoke at meetings of hundreds of students and presented the enormous spiritual needs of the huge nation of China. Hudson was overwhelmed by the response he received—unexpected gifts of money and dozens of volunteers to go to

"GOD IS MOVING... ARE WE ALSO MOVING?"

China. To his utter amazement, when Hudson left for China in October of 1888, fourteen others sailed with him. Once again he marveled at the guidance God had given. If he had once again turned down the invitations to speak in America, he would never have known of the love and eagerness of the American people to help in the work of the China Inland Mission.

After a brief stay in China, Hudson Taylor again visited North America and helped to organize a branch of the China Inland Mission there. Then he traveled on to Sweden and Norway, speaking to as many as 5,000 people at one time. Everywhere he went, people were keenly interested in hearing about China. Even the Queen of Sweden invited Hudson

HE MARVELED AT THE GUIDANCE GOD HAD GIVEN

Taylor for a private audience!

Two things were clear to Hudson Taylor now. First, he should be looking not for seventy or 100 workers, but 1,000 new volunteers for China. Second, these workers would not just come from England but from countries all over the world. Because he strongly believed these two things, Hudson was now more eager to accept invitations to speak and to travel to the far corners of the earth if that was necessary to find 1,000 new workers.

The first trip to America, which he had not been eager to make, had dramatically changed the role Hudson Taylor played with the China Inland Mission. During the next fifteen years he spent less and less time in China and more and more time finding the workers God was sending to carry on the work. He continued visiting the

HE SPENT MORE TIME FINDING THE WORKERS GOD WAS SENDING

United States, Canada, Sweden, Norway, France, Germany, Switzerland, Australia, and New Zealand.

Just as in the early days God had given Hudson Taylor a vision for working in the heart of China, now God had given him a vision for including Christians all around the world in telling the Good News of Jesus Christ to the Chinese people.

GOD HAD GIVEN HIM A VISION !

HUDSON GAZED UPON THE LANDMARKS

12

As the ship glided into the harbor at Shanghai in April of 1905, Hudson Taylor gazed upon the landmarks which had become so familiar over the last fifty years. On his first trip to Shanghai, Hudson had been a young man full of vision and ideals. But he had not known what to expect from living in China. At the age of twenty-one, his heart had burned passionately to tell the Good News of God's love to the Chinese people. He never imagined that his humble work would some day lead to a worldwide organization to send missionaries to China.

Hudson made his way into the city and arrived at the Mission's Shanghai headquarters.

Even before he reached his room he smelled the lovely fragrance of the flowers that filled it. He looked around at the many flower arrangements which welcomed him and he began to read the cards attached. *How kind they all are to share my grief*, he thought to himself.

Hudson had spent the winter in Switzerland mourning the loss of Jennie. She had seemed quite well when the summer began, but later had to spend several weeks in bed. Faithfully and lovingly, Hudson had sat at Jennie's bedside until at last it was obvious she would not recover. It was difficult for her to breathe, and Hudson was in anguish because he could do nothing to help her.

"Ask Him to take me quickly," she had whispered.

"ASK HIM TO TAKE ME QUICKLY"

And Hudson had prayed. He had never had a harder prayer to pray, but for her sake, he cried out to God to free her. Within five minutes, Jennie was gone.

Hudson had stayed in Switzerland through the winter, but when spring came his heart turned again to China. He was no longer General Director of the China Inland Mission, but he felt he could still be a good missionary. China had captured his heart as a boy and had never released its hold.

He was seventy-three years old now, and he knew that traveling in China could be difficult. But he was determined to go. His son, Howard, a medical doctor, and his wife had traveled with Hudson before and they agreed once more to go with him to China.

And so he returned to Shanghai, and from

AND SO HE RETURNED TO SHANGHAI

there traveled to the other places which held special meaning for him. Free of the task of overseeing the Mission, he could instead visit mission stations far away from Shanghai; he could once again travel to the inland provinces of this country he loved.

At Yangchow he took the easy path to the cemetery where Maria and four of their children were buried. It was Easter and rather than feeling sorrowful Hudson's heart was filled with sweet memories: Maria as the gentle young woman he had fallen in love with; Gracie's high voice chattering eagerly; the boys who chased each other and squealed through the house; the tiny baby who had made Maria happy during her last weeks. He had long ago stopped grieving, and now he knew that he would soon be reunited with

HUDSON'S HEART WAS FILLED WITH SWEET MEMORIES

these members of his family.

Next they took a steamship to Hankow, a busy center for the Mission, which was connected to villages lying deep in the heart of China. Hudson visited happily with old friends who had worked in China for half a century.

"Hudson, you have become such a traveler," said one old friend. "But we certainly did not expect you to visit way out here."

"My friend," Hudson replied, "I intend to go on from here. I can never see enough of inland China to satisfy me."

"But you are an old man," his friend teased.

"No older than you," Hudson retorted, "and you are still here."

The expression on his friend's face grew serious. "I could never leave the work. I

"I CAN NEVER SEE ENOUGH OF INLAND CHINA"

could never stay away from China."

"Then you know how I feel," Hudson said, and the two friends stood together sharing a silence which said they understood each other.

In the fifty years since Hudson Taylor's first journey to China many improvements had taken place which made traveling a great deal easier than it had been. The journey from Hankow north to Hunan had once taken two weeks of strenuous, tedious travel. Now the trip was made comfortably in six hours on the sleek, efficient railroad. In the past, visiting five different mission stations around Hunan would have been a major project; now even an old man could travel easily from village to village encouraging generations of Christians.

But even modern travel could not make

NOW THE TRIP WAS MADE COMFORTABLY IN SIX HOURS

Hudson Taylor a young man again. More and more often he was too tired for evening meetings, or even to have supper with his son and daughter-in-law.

"There, Father," Howard said, patting his father's pillow, "that should make you more comfortable. Lie back and rest, and I will get your supper."

Hudson nodded at Howard and smiled at his daughter-in-law, who sat nearby looking at letters from England and a missionary newsletter.

"Aren't these pictures wonderful?" she asked. "I know traveling around makes it hard to keep up with your mail. Perhaps when you feel more rested—"

She stopped in the middle of her sentence when she heard Hudson gasp. She thought

"AREN'T THESE PICTURES WONDERFUL?"

maybe he was going to sneeze, but instead he gasped again. The blank look on his face frightened her.

"Howard!" She ran to the door calling for her husband. "Howard, hurry!"

The end had come.

Howard rushed back into the room just in time to see his father take his last breath. In only a few seconds the weight of seventy-three years in an earthly body passed away; the weary lines in Hudson's face disappeared. He looked like a child quietly sleeping in a peaceful room.

It was not a death that Howard and his wife witnessed. Rather, it was a swift and joyful entry into eternal life. Hudson Taylor bravely ventured on another journey in response to the voice of God.

HUDSON TAYLOR BRAVELY VENTURED ON ANOTHER JOURNEY